GATHERINGS
A COLLECTION OF NORTH CAROLINA POETRY

SPRING STREET EDITIONS
Sylva, North Carolina

Special thanks go to:

The Jackson County Arts Council for financial support; the staff of City Lights Bookstore in Sylva, NC for their support and encouragement; Matt Liddle for help with publication design; and the poets – whose time went not only into the writing but also the production of this book.

First Edition 2001

©2001
Spring Street Editions
3 East Jackson Street
Sylva, NC 28779
828-586-9499

ISBN 0-9712046-0-8

TABLE OF CONTENTS

INTRODUCTION Kathryn Byer · 5
FOREWORD Fred Chappell · 7

MOON ON THE RIVER Beverley A. Cooper · 9
OAK STREET WALTZ Terri Spence · 10
TRANSITION Dawn Clutter · 11
LEAP OF FAITH Cheri Dorondo · 12
WATER Kyle Taylor Barrineau II · 14
KA-BOOM Michael Beadle · 15
QUENCHING NIGHT'S THIRST Chris Boss · 16
SAN JUAN SIN AQUA Ina Claire Bryant · 17
VILLANELLE FOR A BAD DAY Catherine Carter · 18
WE THREE FOR SUPPER Cindy Cavin · 19
VACATION Robert Keith Brown · 20
SOUTHERN MOMENTS Misty Lackey · 20
MONOLOGUE AS SHE DOES THE LAUNDRY Hannah Crane · 21
REALITY Tristen Connor · 22
FUTILITY Virginia Culp · 23
STICKS Becky Curle · 24
YEAR 2000 Louise B. Davis · 25
DARKNESS Chad Disharoon · 26
OUR GIFTS Sylvia Martelli Dobray · 27
IMPRIMATUR FOR PLEASURE Joyce Foster · 28
UNTITLED POEM ON THE SELF James D. Hogan · 29
DOG FIGHT Brian Henderson · 30
UPON ENTERING HUNTER LIBRARY Joe Innis · 31
DREAMS Heather Kelley · 32
CORA Phillip Johnston · 33
MANHATTAN IN MAY Elizabeth A. Kelly · 34
REFLECTIONS UPON KATHLEEN'S DEPARTURE Michelle Martin · 35
CRUISING Nijihia Mbitiru · 36
TO BE READ WITH A SMILE & A LITTLE LAUGH Kate McCarley · 37
STOOD UP ON PROM NIGHT Susan Montalban · 38
WATCHING POTS AT BRASSTOWN Ralph Montee · 39
THE RENTAL LIFE Galadriel Mitchell · 39
PEACE Nancy Nichols · 40
EVERGREEN Jamieson Ridenhour · 41
IF I COULD BE A TREASURE Melody Carol Stallings · 42
PEACE Crystal Olson · 43

INTRODUCTION

When *Word and Witness: One Hundred Years of North Carolina Poetry* was published a year ago, Joyce Moore and I put our heads together and planned a celebration. We knew we wanted to gather local writers featured in the anthology to read from their work at City Lights Bookstore in Sylva, NC. We knew we wanted to draw an audience to the reading, and we wanted to make the point that North Carolina poetry is a living, growing thing, something not easily contained in one state anthology.

So we hatched a plan. Since people like entering contests, we decided to put together a regional poetry competition focused around the anthology, with winners receiving copies of the book. The winners would be announced the night of the reading/booksigning for the anthology and would be invited to read their own winning entries. This sounded like a sure-fire way to draw an audience, and as the entries arrived (all submitted anonymously, by the way), we became excited about the upcoming event.

By deadline, we had received poems from close to 40 local poets. More important, the poems themselves were all worth recognition, and judging was so difficult that we had multiple winners in all categories. We realized that we had accumulated a body of work that deserved to be enjoyed by more than the listeners who gathered for the anthology booksigning.

And so over the past year, we have worked with all the poets involved to draw together a collection that represents the best of the poems submitted. You hold the result of this labor in your hands. We hope it brings you pleasure. And a sense of pride. With this collection, a new century of North Carolina poetry has begun, and it started right here in Jackson County.

KATHRYN BYER

FOREWORD

If you hold a poetry collection at a proper distance from your ear, you'll hear a generalized, busy hum, as of a social gathering in the house next door. Then, if you walk across and open the door, the voices become more distinct and distinctive. Personalities evince their differences in the rhythms of speech, the choices the words make, the colors of voices, the musical flights of phrases. The sound is no longer like that of a beehive or an aviary, but like a consort of musical instruments. For a long time it may seem that the performers are only warming up, tuning their flutes and banjos; the voices seem separate and disconnected. But if you listen attentively for a little while, you may realize that each voice is carrying variations on one of the simultaneously sounded main themes.

So the pages at hand.

It will seem at first that the poet Chris Boss, who observes so carefully a small detail ("A dirty dish / Displaying dried orange pulp – / Crust obscuring the bottom") can have little in common with Kyle Taylor Barrineau, the poet who begins by cataloguing immensities ("The Atlantic is over thirty-one / million miles and rubs / all the American continents"). The poet whose rhythms are "snappin'and tappin' / zippin'and jumpin'" seems to speak a different language from the one who keeps a faithful death watch: "And I see, / at her last breath, the gentle face of the moon passing quietly over the river." One poet rhapsodizes ("Oh, what a wonderful life, What a spectacular day") while another sings the blues ("My fully furnished life, complete with ugly couches / and tacky coffee tables."). How can Michael Beadle and Beverly A. Cooper, Galadriel Mitchell and Kate McCarley have any least concern in common?

Yet soon enough it is obvious that there is a kinship here, that you have entered a gathering of observant, openhearted, broadly intentioned, and intently vocalizing folk, all of them eager to impart knowledge and feeling, to tell you the news and more than the news. It is a gathering different from most other gatherings because of the urgency and depth of import of the conversation, but it is like other gatherings because the people here are like other people. If they were not, they would have little to say worth the hearing. And if you incline your ear closely, you will discover something else – they are not only avid to talk, they are avid, even anxious, to hear what you have to say.

Next time you come, bring your own poems with you.

FRED CHAPPELL

MOON ON THE RIVER

There is really nothing to do except stare through the oval
of the airplane window down at watery lights and lakes and
        dark hills.
Rivers branch the landscape; they connect the smallest
        constellation
of lights to the great flashing city we left, more loyal than any
        road.
The pale circle of the moon flits along black snaking waters.
It follows us, silent and graceful, emerging from a dark forest
like a curious deer. Its face, delicate and serene, dawns
against a cracked mirror, dances out of view. This flight will be
the last long journey to see her. I know of nothing
but to watch my chin on my hand appear in ghostly flickers
like an old film spitting images across a screen, suspended
in space, with the moon racing itself behind.

There is not much you can do for a dying person, but maybe
        talk,
or hold her hand or stroke her forehead. It's even harder
        if all of these
cause her cringing pain, and you can see the brush of your
        fingertips burn
against her lips as you slip an icecube that she cries for,
        like a baby bird,
into her mouth. So we sit our vigil, and tell her
she is loved in low voices.
With each rise and fall of her chest she is farther away, but still
        she is
watching us, intent, with an expression like wonder. And I see,
at her last breath, the gentle face of the moon passing quietly
        over the river.

BEVERLEY A. COOPER

OAK STREET WALTZ

Halfway up the block the heavy bass
thumps my chest.
Sound and light punch a hole in the damp
street darkness, exhaling a vapor
of cigarette smoke and hot beer sweat.
A couple of aging winos rest
their feet in the gutter, warming
themselves next to the music.
I push through a haze of chatter at the bar,
then elbow my way to the stage where

a huge, gold tooth gleaming black man
who ought to be the king of something pumps
a rhinestone accordion. *You got give it to me*, he
roars, while behind him a spider-legged brother
works a washboard over with a pair
of spoons and the guitar player smiles,
sleepy-eyed, like he knows where
you slept last night
and who with.

A long, dark man with
a hard-creased cowboy hat and
a jail tattoo on his forearm flashes me
a grin as he grabs my hand and swings me
out onto the dance floor. We step and
step and turn and step and
his eyes strike sparks against the lilt
of a Cajun waltz and he

becomes every lover I ever had,
every love I ever lost. We press our
bodies and slide our hips
and the squeal and the scrape ease into a
smooth glide, a sweet,
bitter ache in my guts
and my thighs that wheels me

into blood and bone and
teeth and stars until
the last note,

long and slow,
awakens us
together, our skins uneasy with desire,
surprised to find ourselves
strangers.

    TERRI SPENCE

TRANSITION

So subtly, the colors changed
and our world of green was gone.
Hungry eyed, the people came
to banquet on the mountain glory.
"Peak time," it is called.
Gift shops and eating places thrived.
Leaves, the last of them politely staying
for the visitors, now fall eagerly.
Summer residents pack their bags.
"Closed for the Season" signs appear.
Old-timers make predictions.
What color are the wooly worms?
Where is the moss the thickest?
Chimneys are checked and wood piled high.
Bird feeders made ready for the trusting ones.
Suddenly silent, our winter nears.
We welcome it
for spring is out there waiting.

    DAWN CLUTTER

LEAP OF FAITH

Every Wednesday, Sunday morning noon and night,
we parked our pirogues, docked our desires,
and traded sultry for sin, squeezing through the church door
by the skin of our teeth, gnashing, weeping,
and wailing because we had to change our bikinis
for low skirts and high collars. Communion was taken,
penance collected, and we wrung out
our consciences, anticipating God's wrath.

In church, life and death fought for space
in the pews, while the preacher billowed the grey-green folds
of the baptismal curtains, trolling for souls
with the lure of perdition,
the taste of fear not bread
on the water. We squirmed
remembering how freely we swam
just yesterday in the Wilmington. Next door

the neighbors chummed the water
with their sea chaff. All morning
we lingered, floating with the current,
staring up at the sky
thinking of nothing
but the sun strong on us,
and feeling
wet heat close as skin.

We never even considered death
feeding on fishheads
at the roots of the marshgrass,
until it was caught later that day
after we'd climbed out of our frolic.
We'd remember this
as the preacher spoke of life's fragility,
of the soul's delicate nature, shouting

that there was no pure spirit

that is not corrupted
by instinct, by love
of the flesh. For solace,
we'd conjure thoughts of warm rivers
running constantly,
sometimes like a broken faucet
washing our souls away, sometimes
like a gentle stream
of favorite melodies, easy and dulcet,
but never like old-time
honey from a barrel. The sermons drained
away that sweetness from our rivers,
as children wept, their joy
drowned in guilt. Later, I understood
my rivers had always pulled me

strong from that dock. One minute
I'd be floating near salvation. The next,
I was around Turner's bend,
headed for the Caribbean, or India, or Jess's fish camp–
anywhere. So what if we jumped into a river
where we couldn't see the bottom?
It was a leap of faith
we used to joke, the only one I'd ever take.

Cheri Dorondo

WATER

The Atlantic is over thirty-one
million square miles and rubs
all the American continents.
It connects the Americas to Europe
and Africa. There is an undetermined
amount of life within the Atlantic,
as well as a multitude of natural
resources. I am pretty sure no one
has ever successfully swum from America
to Europe.

The Tuckaseegee runs from the mountains
of North Carolina to the Nantahala,
which lends itself eventually to the Atlantic Ocean.
The Tuckaseegee is a weak river
with the highest class rapid reaching almost 2.
The Tuckaseegee has many tributaries.
For example, Dill's Creek runs from Jones Cove
down through Sylva where it meets with the
Tuckaseegee in Dillsboro, NC.
Dill's Creek is small enough that in some places
you can jump right over it.

If you lived on the other side of Dill's Creek,
we could look at the salamanders
and snakes. We could even look
into each other's eyes and talk and laugh.
We could hold hands and walk up and down
for quite some distance.
But, the Atlantic is a different story.
For now, we can just hold hearts
and pretend that the Atlantic
is Dill's Creek, after all, it's the same
water.

KYLE TAYLOR BARRINEAU II

KA-BOOM

Can't sit still, man.
Got these phat rhymes in my head, man.
They got me snappin' and tappin'
    zippin' and jumpin'
        turnin' the whole world
            into somethin'
                Wild!
These rhymes don't just mess around –
    They're precocious and ferocious
        and explocious!
They're ready to set the moon on fire.
They're ready to open all the cages,
    rip out all the pages
    and start
        a whole new book.
So watch out, man.
Here's the message in the bottle:
Hold on to the throttle
    'cause this rocket ship is takin' off!
We're skippin' the countdown.
Tell Houston we've definitely got a problem.
We're about to take every law of science
    and shatter it like a supernova!
'Cause these rhymes in my head, man,
    they make me wanna scream!
        It's like one of those mad Martian dreams.
You know, the one where they keep chasin' after you
    so hard you wish you had more legs.
Man, when these rhymes are racin' through my head,
    they don't have time to switch gears –
They only have one gear – psychocrazy superfurious fast!

So, ladies and gentlemen,
hold on to your socks, hold on to your shoes, hold on to your elbows,
    your earlobes, your car keys, your credit cards, your remote control,

>   your half-paid mortgage, your family tree, your fear of the dark,
>   the beat of your heart, the secret of art, the soul of the start,
>   the flick of the spark,
>   and watch the world go
>   KA-BOOM!

Michael Beadle

QUENCHING NIGHT'S THIRST

    I.
Before dawn
Before night relinquishes its hold on morning
I enter the kitchen
My dry mouth searching for moisture

Holding a glass of orange juice
Up to the lamplight
I turn
Noticing the brilliant reflection in the darkened window

Staring at the window's reflection, drinking the juice
Night steadily yields to dawn as dryness yields to moisture

    II.
Washing dishes three days later,
I reach for the empty glass–
A dirty dish
Displaying dried orange pulp–
Crust obscuring the clear bottom

Chris Boss

SAN JUAN SIN AQUA

Don't tug, muchacha,
      on the clean, white lady's dress

Above a withered earth
Apathy tinged with arrogance
      had etched its way
           across the porcelain visage, pale and kempt
As perfumed patroness dispelled curiosity
      upon a race beset by dust
And plagued with ignorance
      nurtured only by a corn provender.

Yet, across that night to follow,
      uneasiness tinged with distress
           flung its nagging face.
A small, brown hand insistently
      slipped about the lips of Somnus
           thrusting into rumpled dreams
                both anguish and anxiety.

Don't tug, muchacha,
      on the clean, white lady's soul.

INA CLAIRE BRYANT

VILLANELLE FOR A BAD DAY

I can't explain. Today was really bad.
I've lost my journal. Everything is wrong
and thick with misery, as if to add

insult to idiocy; I'm dense and sad
with wretchedness that's loth to bend to song.
I can't explain "today was very bad"

and have it all come clear: the stuffed-in head,
the journal – its loss shivering like a gong
with wasted misery – to which I add

with horseshoe crabs, tossed up but not yet dead
among the rocks and sand, their deaths days long.
They might explain why this day was so bad:

I pulled them from the surf, gleaming like lead
(but still they died) and lifted them and flung
them back to misery. To which I add,

I've lost my words, and seen the armored heads
bleed blue against the riprap. All along –
I can't explain – I knew today was bad
with the whole world's misery. To which we add.

Catherine Carter

WE THREE FOR SUPPER

Sitting in silence
Wondering if the daylight
Will ever come to an end

Watching the old lady drivers
As they try to maneuver
Their big cars into tiny driveways

Listening to the sounds
Of an old empty schoolhouse
That no longer boards children

The gravel flourishes
Into the roadside on the hill
With every passing resident

My mother calls to me
And my little brother
From across the block

He runs across the pebbles
In his little cowboy boots
As I drift along slowly

Miraculously there are no screams
Or foodfights yet either
And my mother is all alone

Sadly I feel myself smile
And mother seems unusually gay
As we three sit down for supper

Cindy Cavin

VACATION

Sand covers my toes.
The sun rests upon my head.
My thoughts are at sea.

    Robert Keith Brown

SOUTHERN MOMENTS

Southern curtains.
Southern sheets.
Southern romance,
In the heat.
Southern coffee.
Southern air.
Breathing, we are always southern's care.

    Misty Lackey

MONOLOGUE AS SHE DOES THE LAUNDRY

I know who shot John Anderson
I know who put an end to Anytown's most prominent man
I have watched him become the exemplary family man
I know how the other ladies looked at his handsome stature
and went into a pitterpat

I know who shot John Anderson
I knew him, the happy and easy man
The all-American, the picture perfect
A true ideal

I know of mistakes in choices
I know of poor judgement in a blind love
I know of the masks that we must wear
I know of the scars we must hide

I know how the blows of a fist feel against my cheek
I know how the cold March wind feels in a lonely house
I know that words are the sharpest knife, just like mamma said
I know how easily dreams are shattered
I know the answer to Anytown's deepest, strangest mystery
I know of what the paper calls "a twisted mind full of anguish"

I know who shot John Anderson
I know who robbed our community of such a fine man
I know who will face the Hotseat in Raleigh

I shall never forget that night in late October
The leaves turning golden
Good night John, I said, one last time
And then I closed my eyes and set myself free...

HANNAH CRANE

REALITY

The walls of my gingerbread house
that I've retreated into for many years
are now beginning to waste away.

Humanity looks me straight in the eyes
and all I can do is gape at life in general
as the ignorance that used to shelter me slowly withers away.

The transparent curtains of innocence have been lifted
and the view is disturbingly unfamiliar.
I wish to forget what I've witnessed.

I used to naively smile at the world
and I'm still curious
as to why it doesn't smile back.

Before harsh reality roused me
I used to dream a lot
but now I'm not quite as confident.

I used to know who I was
but society took its toll
and the inevitable confusion's set in...

    TRISTEN CONNOR

FUTILITY

She rises in the dim of dawn, returns within the dusk;
No one heeds her silent cry, although it seems they must.
She never hints she yearns for more than just a simple task;
Her quiet face may be sincere…more likely it's a mask.

She lies down on her lonely bed – for her there is no rest,
And Rebellion, wild and raging, writhes and tumbles in her breast.
And scenes of useless Conquest rend the darkness with their light,
And the briny tears rush, scalding, o'er her shame beneath the night.

For a moment she is ready, she is strong in all her might!
She anticipates her conquest, for she knows that she can fight!
But the dawn comes grimly creeping, and in the light of day,
She sees all her visions crumble, and the dustman sweeps them away.

She rises in the dim of dawn, returns within the dusk;
No one heeds her silent cry, although it seems they must.
She never hints she yearns for more than just a simple task;
Her quiet face may be sincere…more likely it's a mask.

VIRGINIA CULP

STICKS

Mom's tears prick my ears as I listen
from the other room. I am dumb, small
and cannot get through to her.
I see the pictures of her in hell, yet I stand by
with my hands coiled behind my white back.
Angels hover over her as she writhes
in pain. They promise to never leave
her side. I want to throw a stick
or something. GO AWAY, screaming
does no good. They feed her pills, take x-rays,
hand her pamphlets and all the while
she shakes.

          It does not surprise me anymore, her shaking
        I mean. My teenage brain forgets that she is always at
       war and I cry and pout because she will not
          come with the rest of us
to the movies.

       In college, I am still mad, having time to collect lots of
        nights of pouting. But I wrap my rage up sweetly
         and keep it fresh, releasing it only for
family visits.

      But still they fight her; scratching and ripping at my mother's
       precious flesh. And Somewhere I am thinking
         if my hands were free,
          maybe I could find
those sticks.

BECKY CURLE

YEAR 2000

When computers reach the millennium
They're sure to upset your tum-tum,
Striving your brain to expand
To absorb your computer's demands!

Your software will harden by then
Just remember way back when,
Chips were chopped from a log
Never left your brain in a fog!

A mouse was a creature so small
You worried about legs of your cover-alls
It scurried around through the hall,
Into a hole; and that's all!

2000's a heart beat away
And here's what the experts say,
Things will come to a grinding halt
Computer glitches; it's their fault!

So when we all get to heaven
God's word may be "time out,"
You can't come in by groups of seven
The computer broke down, no doubt!

But, friends, don't worry or fret
The best things are yet to be,
Hearken to God's word, no sweat
We'll triumph and be home free!

Louise B. Davis

DARKNESS

As objects pass through time,
The window of life begins to cast its reflections.
Through the window a face appears.
This face becomes illuminated.
It grows distorted and long.
It becomes shadowed and aged.

A flash of light and it disappears,
Only to reappear in darkness
For this is what life has become.
A life of shadow and decency.
A life of secrets and betrayal.
Appearing only at night.

As the reflection reveals itself further
It loses its color.
It shifts from blue to green,
And finally attains the color of white and black.
The skin becomes bone and the eyes hollow obscurity.
Eventually the shadows disappear and so to the face
With only a blinding light burning from above.

This heavenly light finally subsides.
The shadows reclaim their reflection but without the face.
The face has now become only a memory.
A memory of light.
A memory of darkness.
A memory that exists within the mind of mortal men.
Only to wither away and die,
As darkness lies deep within light.

CHAD DISHAROON

OUR GIFTS

In many lands, in many homes the Christmas bells won't ring
In many lands, in many homes no carols will they sing.
They know not of our Savior's birth not how the angels sang,
Peace on Earth Good Will to Men, those loud hosannas rang.
They know not how He sent His Son on that bright Christmas day
How can they know, how can they see, unless we lead the way.
So as this time of Christmas Joy draws nearer by the day
We humbly bring our loving gifts, and at their feet we lay
With it, our prayer to Thee oh God, our Great Redeemer, Lord and King
Bring peace within their hearts today so that they too may sing…

      Of the Silent Night so long ago, upon a Midnight Clear
      In the Little Town of Bethlehem, Herald Angels so near
      Singing Joy to the World, for our Savior now is born
      Away in a Manager on that bright Christmas morn.
      Three Wise Men also came paying homage to their King
      Gold, Frankincense and Myrrh, these gifts they did bring

Our prayer for those this day, who know not of this story
Is that the giver of the greatest gift, in all His matchless Glory
Will use the warmth of our love to melt these gifts that lay
Into a bright and shining star to lead them to the only way
Of everlasting love and life that only He can give
So like we who have heard, they too may hear, believe, obey and live!

SYLVIA MARTELLI DOBRAY

IMPRIMATUR FOR PLEASURE

I dance alone to the blues
swinging on the satin covered notes
     of B.B. King.
Fingers caressing the ivory keys
erase the lines from my
     weathered face
and I am a feather boa swaying
    to brass horns blowing,
a saucy calico strutting
   to jazz drums beating.

I dance alone in a home free
     of prison brawls
where once, during sullen truces,
we picked up pieces of fractured psyches
    and bits of heart
blown apart in sudden clashes.

I dance alone circling through
     the rooms
like a toy boat unmoored floating
    on a garden pond,
an unfettered balloon drifting
    in soft air
listening to ole B.B. sing about
    a blues man, a good man,
and I'm wanting one, understand,
but for now this dance is taken.

    JOYCE FOSTER

UNTITLED POEM ON THE SELF

In this morning's rain
I saw him walking. In
      navy blue

Taking the road less taken
I found him from the office window
      contrasting against the leaves
           orange contrasting cold

I imagined him walking
                        on the shore
              on the bluff
                  in the flatland, near the mounts

Of course there's no escape
the black void
closing in
            Have the cities corrupted?
                Has innocence been lost?
    No.

But he represents progress
Thanks to Jeffers,
            He wishes to reverse progress.
Solitary.
      Alone.
           Apart from society.

From the office window...
in this morning's rain.

JAMES D. HOGAN

DOG FIGHT

Hang gliding personas talk airily
until they reach that one spot,
you know, over the paper mill
where they all scream in unison,
"I'll shoot your dog!"

The manager of the plant
looks up confused, "I –
don't have a dog."
The aerial antagonists huddle
for a moment as they put their guns away.

"Here's the plan," one says,
"We'll give him a dog tomorrow."
They smack each other
on the back and leave
a sinister trail
of laughter that drifts
slowly to the ground behind them.

Brian Henderson

UPON ENTERING HUNTER LIBRARY

You reach the doors and stop.
Your eyes are met with a beautiful afternoon.
A soft blue sky accompanied by cotton-ball clouds
brings a certain inner peace to this lovely day.
Song birds heard from nearby trees,
light breeze blows through your hair,
standing it up,
setting it back down.
You smile at this, but your smile slowly fades into a look of
                uncertainty.
And you turn around to face those doors;
those doors which mock everything around you;
those doors which open to another world,
the thought of time a mere insult to their existence.
Beyond those doors your quest for knowledge begins...

You find that you are not alone.
There are others on their own quest,
their restless souls scattered, searching different isles,
sitting here and there trying to find that knowledge,
not realizing that finding that knowledge only leads to an
                endless search of another.
Their faces are masked with determination, frustration, fear, and confusion.
A concrete mold that has dried in a series of violent twists.
A low roar of whispers and turning pages can be heard throughout,
the constant sound of waves crashing against the shore.

Descending stairs,
your footsteps offer only echoes of laughter,
surrounded by portraits of intimidation which look down upon you,
their piercing eyes reminding you of your unworthy presence,
thoughts of surrender begin to unfold, pushed back by an unknowing confidence;
a confidence that can only come from the deepest depths of your undying soul,
you come face to face with fear itself, not realizing what awaits on the other side;
a doorway to the rest of your life...
You pass through,
greeted by a thick blanket of silence,

a silence so overwhelming;
a silence that seems to grab your entire helpless body in its cold hand.
On either side, as you wade through this thick silence, rows of accomplishments taunt you with
their patient existence,
daring you to challenge what has already been said,
challenging you to dare others to challenge what you have yet to say.
You take the dare,
accept the challenge,
as you place yourself among the silence of words,
racing against time, which doesn't exist.

    JOE INNIS

DREAMS

Under a star speckled sky I sit
Upon a rocky and jagged red cliff
And stare at the blackening blue-silver sky

Reaching out I want to touch the stars
Hold one in the palm of my hand
Blow gold moondust off the surface
To watch it sparkle upon my skin

My legs dangle over the airless edge
Reaching down into endless oblivion

    HEATHER KELLEY

CORA

She was impoverished,
The kind that destroys confidence over a lifetime of discrimination.
She was long and spindly
She had bad teeth,
   and at the slightest note of confidence would
      lower her eyes,
      move hands into pockets,
      and shield herself with her right shoulder and elbow.

She struggled up on the house late that summer
I saw her through the window
I moved quickly and spoke with loud hospitality
      crushing what strength she had gained.
She pointed up the hill with her free hand,
      as if justifying her presence, and muttered "Neighbor"
I smiled uncomfortably
      It must have been contagious
She handed me a bowl of beans,
      "from the garden," she spilled out, and nodded before escaping.

They sat in my icebox
Spoiled
and when I threw them out,
      I knew I could not appreciate their value.
Each bean picked
Slow cooked
Meant to make a friendship warm.

I prayed hard on those beans
Thought about how lost I was.

Fall passed on by,
      and at first snow I found wood piled on the step...

I walked up the hill
Fluffed snow flakes on my shoulders,
And the smell of soup beans rolled from the pot
      in clouds of warm friendly steam.

PHILLIP JOHNSTON

MANHATTAN IN MAY

Towering gray buildings,
With wet washed windows like
      Quick silver
Reflecting hot white rays,
      Hover over street people:
The theatergoers and art critics.

I have seen this world from
Outside, standing before the busy mote
      Past ancient stone walls
Bearing names and dates for
Those who came before;
      They laid the foundation
And sleep an easy rest among
The mended fences: their manicured plots.

Now, at night when children cry
While cathedral bells chime,
      Your thousand blinking eyes
Glare on the blue black back-drop
Past the Long Island Sound
      Loosing their vision in the
Palest green light born of an
Uncommon open sky.

    ELIZABETH A. KELLY

REFLECTIONS UPON KATHLEEN'S DEPARTURE

She will walk free,
to see all the world has to give.
While those bound and chained to an American Dream
frown upon her.
But she smiles and laughs,
knowing she is probably fulfilling her vocation
more than I.
Who sits here
head crammed in a book
Slaving and waiting for a piece of paper
that suddenly makes me
more eligible.
Eligible, to make my mark
from nine to five.
Eligible, to be the fool
selling my time for gold.
But they have knowledge.
A wisdom.
No institution can teach.
You must learn from others,
then build your own school.

    MICHELLE MARTIN

CRUISING

Hey, what's that I see? Why it's a car,
It's late and there on up is bright Dog Star,
There to guide my crew and me,
Once we're seated, I'll be lost in glee.

So now we're cruising down the road
The streetlamps like lights of gold
And a shade or two of dark dealing
But it's no stab on happy feeling.
Ahead, there's another car: bright, red,
With happy faces, shouts and screams;
Now that's a car that's really fled.
Faster now, with groove on play,
Mellow sounds to smooth out dark day,
And now the firewells have sadly left,
Tucked down in some dark cleft
Waiting for the morrow born in red,
Or the bash, just five minutes ahead.

It's a fast car and us
Top down, sound smooth, lights dim,
On and on, till the urban rim,
Where maybe we might stop and fill
Our gasping tank, air cold, and in kinetic still,
Trees waving, crickets shrill.
Then it's back to the Core
Back for some more
Bashes fast and forlorn:
Before you know it, they're all gone.
So I'll stick to cruising:
The ride in between-
The joyful flux,
The stage when absolutely nothing sucks;
When we are free,
And all the nightshades we haply see
Hoping for many more rides like this,
When we're coasting in metal bound bliss.

NJIHIA MBITIRU

TO BE READ WITH A SMILE & A LITTLE LAUGH

And, there went I,
into the afternoon,
trailing the last thing you said
after me,
like a puppy on a string
or a broad blue ribbon.
Was my hair fire red in the retiring sun?
Did I cock my head just so?
Was I very pretty
as I crossed the intersection
with a smile and a little laugh?
Traffic was so heavy
I had to run.
My arms orbited around me
like an archaic diagram
of the Milky Way.
I almost lost my grace to the gutter.
Oh, what a wonderful life,
What a spectacular autumn day.
I'll see you soon enough,
Or
 At least that's what you say.

Kate McCarley

STOOD UP ON PROM NIGHT

My grandmother gave me a porcelain doll
for my birthday when I turned
seven years old.
My mother never let me play with it.
She put it in a glass case
against the wall of the living room.
That was ten years ago.
It feels like forever,
but she's still there.
She has curly brunette hair,
just like mine.
My favorite color has always been blue.
Grammy knew that,
so she picked a doll all
dressed in blue.
It looks like
smudged eye shadow.
She's so pretty, but all she can do
is stand in that case
like a wallflower,
wearing a veil of dust,
and wait for nothing.
When I was younger,
I used to wonder what it would be like
to be that beautiful doll
protected by the case,
watching everything that goes on
around me.
We are both fragile,
but I am the one who is already
broken.

SUSAN MONTALBAN

WATCHING POTS AT BRASSTOWN

In the kiln at 1700 degrees
glowing bright orange
all pots look the same.
When pots and flame are one
joined in fiery genesis
waiting to happen
the time has come to part them.
As the pots are liberated
from the fire,
there is always a surprise.
My friend the potter says
the best are happy accidents
the worst, broken dreams
that cannot tell you
what has gone before
what may come next.

    Ralph Montee

THE RENTAL LIFE

The smoke swirls attract
       my attention
and the plaid pattern
      on the couch
         The ugly couch.
My fully furnished life,
complete with ugly couches
 and tacky coffee tables.

    Galadriel Mitchell

PEACE

If our world would realize
Love is the missing key
To bring peace on this earth
If only all could see.
To love one another
Reach out a helping hand
Share with each other
We'd see peace in this land.
Put aside an angry heart
Disagree lovingly
Rid ourselves of prejudice
How wonderful 'twould be.
If we could freely give
Instead of want or take
What a difference
In our world would make.
Do our very best to work
To earn our keep and way
Rather than to rob or steal
Never more a prison stay.
If we could live side by side
Have respect for another's life
Lay our guns and ammo down
Put an end to worldly strife.
Harbor not greed or hate
Or wish we had more and more
Be satisfied with what we have
Wouldn't need to fight a war.
Very simple 'twould seem to be
In a world that is so cruel
To bring peace among its people
Is to apply the "Golden Rule."
We love our neighbors as ourselves
Very happy we all would be
Oh if everyone could see
Love is the missing key!

NANCY NICHOLS

EVERGREEN

my grandfather
drives
through the night
while his wife
my grandmother
cooks
soups brimming
with the garden
peas and potatoes
and fresh snap beans
biscuits
spilling butter-steam
across the walls
while history joins
hands 'round the table

when my grandfather
returns
he will smell of long miles and gasoline
and he will sit in the kitchen
wreathed
with cigarette smoke
and talk with her

I perch
on a stool
by the counter
my legs
swinging
two feet above the tile
waiting for pecan pie
and in this time
this place
it is enough
to wait

JAMIESON RIDENHOUR

IF I COULD BE A TREASURE

If I could be a treasure
And choose my hiding place
I would be a song
Of beauty, joy, and grace
And dwell within the heart and soul
Of all God's precious creatures
With flowing tunes and tender words
Love would shine through all their features
So if I were this treasure
This song of love and peace
I'd need to be acknowledged
And never told to cease

MELODY CAROL STALLINGS

PEACE

The rains have come to heal the land;
To rejuvinate our country from strand to strand.
Our hearts are revived, we cry no more
For with sunset's gold, we see heaven's shore.

Our scattered memories are a treasure forever
For no force of nature has the power to sever
This precious jewel called remembrance
In which all bonds of love give us deliverance.

From the tears we cry to the condolences we give
From our mixed emotions to our will to forgive
All of these feelings are a part of God's will
To show us the way, to train us to heal.

Time will take you along torturous trails
And up mountains high and across grassy dells.
Across lakes and streams and stormy seas
Through lands full of darkness and disease.

This journey across the land called Time
Will teach you more than reason or rhyme.
And in the end – when all is done
You will bask in the glory of the setting sun.

    CRYSTAL OLSON

KYLE TAYLOR BARRINEAU II *is a native of Sylva. He lives in New York where he works in the theater.*

MICHAEL BEADLE *is a poet and freelance writer living in Waynesville. He teaches creative writing classes at Central Haywood High School and Haywood Community College.*

CHRIS BOSS *has an MA in English from Western Carolina University where he currently teaches Freshman Composition. He resides in Sylva with his wife.*

ROBERT KEITH BROWN *lives in Cullowhee, NC.*

INA CLAIRE BRYANT, *known as "Sam" and a resident of Sylva, NC, is a great-grandmother, former high school and college teacher of English. Once a wine & cheese shoppe owner in Charlotte, NC, she is a native of Charleston and Darlington, SC.*

CATHERINE CARTER *has work appearing or upcoming in* The Lyric, The Southern Anthology, Green Fuse, Mudfish, Sulphur River Literary Review, Comstock Review, *and* Alligator Juniper, *among others, and as a feature page in* Chiron Review. *She currently has a manuscript circulating,* The Memory of Gills. *She lives and works in Western North Carolina.*

CINDY CAVIN *has lived in Western North Carolina on and off for about 13 years. She is a graduating senior at WCU, majoring in Communication-Electronic Media with a minor in Creative Writing. Her favorite poet is Jim Carroll, her favorite book of all time,* A Catcher in the Rye.

DAWN CLUTTER *was born in Bend, OR in 1920 and spent 49 years of marriage in Ohio, raised 6 children, a busy life. Nine years ago, she moved to NC. Last year she revisited her longed-for Oregon and realized the NC mountains are all she asks. "Transitions" is one of a series of 12 poems entitled "Smoky Mountain Year."*

TRISTEN CONNOR *was born in Newport, RI on January 9, 1985. She was 15 years of age when the poem in this collection was written. She is currently a student in Sylva, NC.*

BEVERLY COOPER *has taught English at Western Carolina University and published poems in many magazines including* Asheville Poetry Review.

HANNAH CRANE *is a native of Highlands, NC. Her influences are Walt Whitman, Joyce Carol Oates, the Beatles and summer nights watching the stars come out while listening to the crickets' serenade.*

VIRGINIA CULP *is a Senior at WCU with a major in English (Professional Writing). Her hometown is Long Creek, SC. She is the 2000-2001* Nomad *editor (WCU's literary magazine).*

BECKY CURLE *is a student at Western Carolina University.*

LOUISE B. DAVIS *is a Senior citizen, born in Jackson County. She graduated from Sylva Central High. Of Baptist or Methodist faith, she sings with Goldenaires and does volunteer work.*

CHAD DISHAROON *is currently a student attending WCU.*

SYLVIA MARTELLI DOBRAY *is 83 years old and has taught Sunday School since she was 19 years old. This poem was written for her Sunday School class of Juniors to encourage them to give to others as God gave to us.*

CHERI DORONDO *was born and raised in the Georgia low country and earned a* degree in comparative literature from University of South Carolina. She spent some years in Europe doing research and studying languages. She has taught at WCU and is now writing seriously, something she wanted to do long ago when she studied with James Dickey. Her chapbook of poems was a finalist in the Persephone Prize contest last year.

JOYCE FOSTER retired to the mountains a number of years ago, discoveing poetry during her mid-sixties at a difficult point in her life. Writing poetry gives her a great deal of comfort and pleasure.

BRIAN HENDERSON has lived in Western North Carolina since 1997 and currently teaches writing at WCU. He likes to experiment with genres, and reputable sources claim that his latest batch of diabolical creations is dangerously close to fruition. Henderson makes no comment, but there is a dark twinkle in his eye.

JAMES D. HOGAN was born in Freehold, NJ and currently resides in Statesville, NC. He attends Western Carolina University pursuing a degree in Secondary Education in English.

JOE INNIS portrays himself as "just the average Joe."

PHILLIP JOHNSTON is a full-time potter in Balsam, NC. He has been published in several micro magazines around the country, and writes mainly to express the beauty and amazing diversity he sees in the people around him.

HEATHER KELLEY is a student at Western Carolina University.

ELIZABETH A. KELLY is a native of Atlanta, GA. She received her BA in English from Piedmont College in Demorest, Georgia. While working on her undergraduate degree, she served as assistant editor for the Habersham Review, a literary journal dedicated to Southern literature. Currently, Ms. Kelly is working on her Master's in English at Western Carolina University and plans on pursuing a Ph.D in rhetoric and composition.

MISTY LACKEY has been writing poetry since 1995. Her first poem published was called "Silence." Since then she has had 39 published and in 1996, a poem "A Moment of Life" won $750.00. She loves to write about anything that creates an image that will inspire others. Her favorite poets are Robert Frost and Edgar Allan Poe.

MICHELLE MARTIN is an English student at WCU, plays guitar, practices tai-chi and shaolin, and enjoys being in nature.

NIJIHIA MBITIRU is a Kenyan student currently studying at Western Carolina University. He has an extensive collection of unpublished poetry he'd like to share with the whole world.

KATE McCARLEY is a native of Sylva who is living and working in Marbella, Spain.

GALADRIEL MITCHELL is a senior at WCU majoring in English with professional writing concentration, an aspiring writer. She is mother to a wonderful daughter, Chloe.

SUSAN MONTALBAN is an English major at Western Carolina University. She has served on the staff of Nomad literary magazine, and is a member of Sigma Tau Delta and English Club.

RALPH MONTEE has worked in sustainable agriculture, environmental and community development internationally for many years. He recently retired from the office of International Programs and Services at WCU.

NANCY NICHOLS says "The mountain truly is my sanctuary. My husband Dick and I have lived here in a log house on Dick's Creek for 4 years now. I have been writing poetry since 1971 and have published one book and written two more. It is a hobby I enjoy and thank my Heavenly Father for giving me everyone."

CRYSTAL OLSON is a sophomore Chemistry major at WCU. She wrote PEACE as a reaction to the shootings at Columbine High School. She was born and raised in Hickory, NC.

JAMIESON RIDENHOUR, a Florence, SC native, moved to Asheville, NC in 1993. During his seven years there, he has been a writer, actor, songwriter, counselor, teacher, and director of a runaway shelter, often all on the same day. As a singer and songwriter, Jamie has released two albums on the Open Door label: "Sensitive Singer-Songwriter Live at the green door" and "No Good Reason". Jamie lives near Asheville in a cabin by a stream with his wife, Gwyn, their son Ian, and two precocious dogs. He recently finished his MA in English at Western Carolina University where he studied poetry under Kathryn Stripling Byer.

TERRI SPENCE is a graduate of WCU, with a major in English. She served as editor of Nomad in 1998-99.

MELODY CAROL STALLINGS is a student at Western Carolina University.